PRAISE FOR STEVEN WILLIS

"Steven Antoine Willis uses his craft to highlight the multi-dimensional nature of Blackness by pairing politics with personal experience. *A Peculiar People* is succinct and focused but simultaneously addresses a wide range of topics such as family, music, hardships, and sacrifice. This book is insightful, brave, humorous and absolutely worth reading."

—RUDY FRANCISCO, AUTHOR OF *I'LL FLY AWAY*

"*A Peculiar People* is a declaration of love for Steven's Blackness, family and life. It serves us grief, joy, and pain on the same plate without hesitation or apology. This collection is both bruise and salve. It is a mirror and a map. It is breathtaking and willful. Steven Willis has surely established himself as a momentous voice in contemporary poetry."

—YESIKA SALGADO, AUTHOR OF *CORAZÓN*

"Steven Willis' work is brilliant in how it depicts Black folks as a special people that goes against the normative grain. Willis, himself, is quite peculiar in how he seamlessly plays with different forms, "non-form," and various modes of language in ways that would impress most any writer. *A Peculiar People* is familiar to those who know and are of the people and wonderfully odd because it discusses Black personhood in ways that aesthetically and politically reject white ways of peopling."

—JAVON JOHNSON, *AIN'T NEVER NOT BEEN BLACK*

"*A Peculiar People* meshes a deft understanding of traditional verse form and a deep reverence for the complexity of Black life that echoes the groundbreaking work of Gwendolyn Brooks' *Annie Allen*. If poems are flexible things that can live in air or on any manner of page, then Steven Willis is a world traveler intent on showing us everywhere his poems can survive and thrive. The infusion of hip-hop sensibility and sentiment display for all a deep emotional intelligence at the center of this book. Wow. This is a worthy first effort from a promising and versatile artist."

—NATE MARSHALL, AUTHOR OF *FINNA*

A PECULIAR PEOPLE

A PECULIAR PEOPLE

poems by Steven Willis

Button Publishing Inc.
Minneapolis
2022

◇

Published by Button Poetry / Exploding Pinecone Press
Minneapolis, MN 55403 | http://www.buttonpoetry.com

◇

All Rights Reserved
Manufactured in the United States of America
Cover design: Nikki Clark
ISBN 978-1-63834-023-2
26 25 24 23 22   1 2 3 4 5

Dedicated to them *damn Willises*
&
anyone who knew me as a boy at 1435 W. 104th St.

For the *Yellow* that came along at my most blue,

I owe you.

In Memory of Georgia Mae Willis

America's **peculiar** institution
—a euphemism used for American slavery popularized by
South Carolina Senator John C. Calhoun.

"But ye are a chosen generation, a royal priesthood, a holy nation, **a peculiar people;** *that ye should shew forth the praises of him who hath called you out of darkness into his marvelous light."*
—*1 Peter 2:9*

CONTENTS

A PECULIAR PEOPLE

a meditation on contemporary
Black personhood

SECTION 1:

PROVERBS

IN SUMMER WE SACRIFICE OUR BOYS TO THE SUN

perhaps it is easier for me to think of the violence in this way, not as

senseless but as a sacrifice to a darker god

one as bronze as we are

a harkening to a forgotten past

where we make ritual out of the surest thing. death

is the sun dance of the ghetto

bodies as dark as night bleed their own sunsets so the sun will shine

i admit i too have prayed for summers

as long as prison sentences   forgetting

an everlasting summer is nothing

short of genocide

BIG MAMA ROOTS FOR EVERYBODY BLACK WHEN
WATCHING WHEEL OF FORTUNE

No exceptions.
She picks her people
before the first toss-up is even finished.

Somebody to shout the answer to
or tell when to solve or to buy a vowel,
to sanctify their spins
with 40 years of game show experience.

If ain't nobody Black
she'll throw her support on somebody *close enough.*
A Gonzalez, Ramirez, or Vargas,
the rare Lee or Yang.

If the pickings are slim,
an episode with contestants white as Vanna,
she'll settle on somebody from *home—*
A Chicago native or
at least somebody from *around the corner:*
a homemaker from Detroit,
the balding plumber from Minnesota,
or the teacher from Wisconsin.

If not, she will sift through the bios
looking for something familiar:
a sick parent, a disabled child, a dream once
too expensive or far-fetched, now
only possible here, on America's
favorite game show,
where only the RSTLNE are given.

HILLARY CLINTON 2008

Nah, you saw first chance he got
he threw Jeremiah Wright under the bus.
I don't trust him.

> He too new. I'm voting for somebody
> who know what they doing.
> Plus she got Bill wit her.

He Black but he ain't Black, Black.
Harvard and Hawaii? Kenya and Kansas?
What he know about what we been through?

> He a safe Black man.
> You see they wasn't gone put Jesse in there.
> A damn shame.

> This nigga just expect to get my vote
> 'cause he Black.

> He lucky
> his wife a sista
> or I wouldn't even entertain his ass.

He ain't gone last the first day in office.

I wouldn't be surprised if one of the Secret Servicemen do it.

> They gone give his ass that JFK special.

> I ain't getting my hopes up,
> you know white folks don't let us have nothin'

WHEN MY INCOME TAX COME

Pay that extra 200
that I owe the landlord.
Tell Momma hold off
I'mma pay her what I owe her.

I make good on all my bets
I ain't trying not to pay
But I need to help my sista'
get that stuff off layaway.

Get the kids some school clothes
to get Trina off my back.
Got to change them tires
and fix the Cadillac

I'mma do something for me
relax and have some fun
And I'mma do it all
when my income tax come.

TO BE CALLED LIL'

means you got a daddy
means your daddy still around
means you know yo cousins on your daddy side
and they know you too

means a man claimed you,
supported you with or without a court's order
means you know nothing of deadbeat
of absentee

means you inherited something
when the block speaks of you, they will say
that's Steve boy. whaddup lil' Steve!

and no they couldn't have called you Junior
because we know Black boys are never young
we are born suspicious and already running

and no they couldn't have called him Senior
because we know Black men never grow old
just threatening and never early for anything

but death

too poor for trust funds
so he gave you what he could
a face
a reputation
his name

HAL.LE.LU.JAH (NOUN) 1. relief or gratitude: as in *Hallelujah, Momma's cancer is gone* or *Hallelujah it ain't much but at least we got something.* 2. a miracle; the unexpected; just in the nick of time: as in *The woman touched the hymn of his garment and Hallelujah! She was healed.* 3. sarcasm; said in vain: as in *Hallelujah! Shirley finally did what was best for her and came to church.* 4. an utterance; praises be to God or to God be the glory.

we never needed a reason to do that.

WHAT TO DO IF THIS HAPPENS

If ever you are startled while in slumber
by a Motown artist's sweet serenade,
and the suck and scream of vacuum cleaner
as the day is commenced
with the ceremonious crackle of the collection of crumbs

GET UP!

It is Saturday morning
and Momma intends to clean.

A WITNESS: CHOOSE YOUR OWN ADVENTURE
after Patricia Smith

Walking out of an elevator in the Parkway Gardens you see a man shoot another man. The police come to you and ask you what you saw.

Turn to page 9 if you ain't see shit.

That's right. It costs you nothing not to see
shit. I mean, you may catch a lil' pressha'
from the narcos, DAs, and CPD.
All guilting you like you shot the nigga,
beggin' you to do the right thing. To think
about the family, and what they need,
'bout peace, justice, the killer in the clink.
How no snitchin' is a terrible creed.
But don't no police come back home with you.
Ask you to take the stand but ain't there when
your body fall. What you think we gone do?
Mind our business. Go on like we been.
We step over your body, let it rot.
You go 'round witnessin shit, you get got.

WISHES FOR THE RICH

after Lucille Clifton

I wish them more mouths to feed
I wish them no hot water
I wish them a petty landlord
I wish them a pack of noodles
with the seasoning packet missing
I wish them tonight's dinner still frozen in the freezer
I wish them no McDonald's money
I wish them no income tax check
I wish them paid on the 1st
I wish them broke by the 3rd
I wish them a baby daddy
who is no help and won't answer the phone
I wish them expensive childcare
I wish them an aching body
I wish them longer hours
I wish them exhaustion
and then
I wish them an extra shift,
the graveyard.

COUNTY COUSINS

So, this one here is for my County Cousins.
Currently incarcerated for crimes committed
and or confessed
contributing to the new Jim Crow.

My County Cousins,
not to be confused with my country cousins
currently in Kansas cooking corn bread
and collard greens in the kitchen.
Those cousins you see every summer
these cousins you see every quarter century.

In county, constantly making collect calls
inquiring about commissary. Cursed
to forever circulate in and out of this country's
industrial prison complex, constructed
for collecting coons
in an orange and black continuum.

My cousin
use to wear busted jeans
to Grandma's Christian church in Chatham.

My cousin
was cool enough to make the most siddity girl crack
a smile.

Was the same cousin
I saw clinch a clutch in rage
at the sight of his brother's blood on concrete,
made that gun cry for days.

Until one day,
a crooked Chicago cop came
and caged my cousin before college,
and now my family only congregates in courtrooms.

I can hear the jury concluding the caucus
that can decide his fate,
but I can't concentrate.
All I can do is think about when we were kids,
and how we use to play cops and robbers on the corner,
and the pleasure I got
each time my cousin was caught
and placed in imaginary cuffs.

But now guilt creeps my conscience,
for I am no different
from these cops turned klansmen,
for how quickly
I was willing to make a criminal
out of my kin.

Maybe I could have called more,
reminded him of the summers we spent
consuming carousels and cotton candy.

My cousin was a fragile child
who'd hear thunder strike and cry to cuddle,
who'd make Big Mama colorful creations,
until only crumbs were left of his Crayolas.
That's who he is,

not the creature who the Counsel called "capital murderer"
claiming he's responsible for this carcass.
Not even Cochran could convince me
my cousin was capable of killing anyone.

Who would have thought that before my cousin
could finesse Father Time out an 18th candle
or convince clocks and calendars to give him
the combination to eternity,
that his life would become a compilation of tears?

Cause now my momma cry
when the gavel cry

and our people cry
when the cuffs cry

and 'nem folks cry
when them bars cry

and I cry
and I cry
and I cry

till my grandmother sighs
and say

quit that crying boy.
Better he be in county
than a casket.

THE CLEAN UP WOMAN RESPONDS

for Betty Wright

I'm not your ruin chile
I'm not y'all undoin chile

When you were out havin' fun,
What you think he was doin' chile?

You blame the other woman
As if we do the pursuin' chile

But a man don't need no help
When he do his foolin' chile

Heartbreak is a rite of passage for us
Ask yo momma, it's been proven chile

Ole Clean Up know you lose em how you get em,
It will be my turn soon then chile

ODE TO THE BOYS WHO ONCE PUSHED MIXTAPES

You were the phoenix to rise from Tupac's ashes
A Rakim reincarnate
With *God's Son* across the belly
the holy one
with hands of bronze and hair of wool
a neck of rope

   gold

yo mama's Brooklyn basement be your tomb

your pitch: you are
the light
a New Testament Emcee
Here to save the culture
from the depths of industry darkness
see some false prophets just wanted to make it rain
but you were a fisher of men

your burnt cd
beckoning me
like a burning bush
on a crowded sidewalk on State Street

You are a forgotten holy.

JOHN 3:16 MAKES AN APPEARANCE

as bumper sticker on your neighbor's minivan,

as bookmark from the local Christian bookstore,

etched on the side of a pencil.

as decor

draped across your grandmother's shower curtain
floormat or tombstone.

Then again. *Given*

as a gift to you from your mother

as wall art for your dorm room or office

on the side of the tote bag the cute girl takes to Trader Joe's.
The words appear

as the only thing not chipped on your father's
oldest coffee mug

still there, but fading
sticker on your coworker's water bottle.

Then again. *Everlasting*

as the first scripture you learned as a child,

as the only verse you can still recite from memory,

pressed on
a T-shirt you got at a youth revival in your teens
now only worn to the gym.

Then again. *Begotten*

in the rare moments of prayer
during the hardest times

as a sign

you still believe.

BLACK FOLK DON'T HAVE BIRTHDAYS

We have birthday weekends,
birthday weeks,
birthday months,

A milestone year like 30 or 50
can result in a yearlong jubilee
of saying *yes* to all pleasures.

As the descendants of the once enslaved,
who had no record of when they were born
and no means by which to celebrate,
we are blessed with the inheritance of extra days.

They whisper,

celebrate child.
Take all the time
you need

THE HUSTLE SPEAKS (MONOLOGUE)

Hey you.
You hear me talking to you.
Look at me.

                                                   Look at me.

What?
              You think you're just going to ignore me?
                  Nobody ignores me.

Too busy listenin' to those politicians and those preachers
tellin' you that I'm trouble.
                                The hustle ain't no trouble.

                       I'm a gift,
                    an escape,
           an opportunity for economic freedom,
            a legitimate chance for people like you.

What kind of man just sits by and lets his mother work her fingers to
                                            the bone
                  slaving at some 9 to 5?

A real man carries his own weight,
or at least pushes it.

                      What do I do?
                I turn D boys into Made Men.
            Offer them bricks so they can build
                something of themselves,
           and you're just going to ignore me?

      You could be running this whole block by now following me.

I've fathered moguls

Frank Lucas, Nicky Barnes, billionaire Jay-Z,

nigga you could own the Roc.

I run everything around this motherfucka'.
I'm the plug.
I provide everything
even the pipe dreams.

That's why ballplayers pass the *rock*
and the rappers *cook it up* in the lab.

I'm the *base*line in that jazz,
the *rock* and that roll

and I'm always in the background
when shit goes up in *smoke.*

I'm the culture.

I'm the reason all the real niggas you know are pushing
whips, bricks, or daisies.

Gave your people more lines than the Bible.
Puff Puff pastor.

How you gon' ignore your God?
Glorify me.

I be the Don da.
The holy ghost of blow smoke.
The chief rocka,
a father to the fatherless.

I gave the abandoned bandits bandos and bands.

I gave them hope.
                    I gave them dope.

Don't you know all you ever gone have is the hustle?

The crack rock be your only inheritance.
                                The corner your only heirloom.

Your grandmother was a user,
your granddaddy was a dealer,
          you got ancestors on both sides of the transaction nigga,
                    you got the hustle in your genes.

You gone ignore me even though you hungry boy?
                          Even though the water bill past due,
                                and the light and gas too?
Ain't you tired of getting bullied at school?
                          Don't you want a new pair of shoes?

I've given you everything to make you a supreme level hustla'

a deadbeat daddy and a well-to-do mother
                                    the failing schools
the unsafe neighborhoods
                    the second-class skin
and the streets
just crawling with fiends

just begging for you
to come into yourself

now come into yourself
boy, come into yourself

                    and take your place
                          at my mighty right hand.

THINGS TO DO WITH THE EVICTION NOTICE
BESIDES LEAVE

1. Use as scratch paper to write my rhymes
2. Use as bookmark in my Bible
3. Smash these roaches
4. Stash my roaches
5. Roll up
to smack the dog's nose with
6. Paper airplane
7. Ignore it
and make them Sheriff come take home from me.

(EAST) BEVERLY HILLS, CHICAGO
a failed golden shovel.

We are a generation removed
from the piss puddle in the elevator.
Managed a little more than a pot to piss in,
but *nobody*

gave us anything.
Our children are born with a silver spoon,
an heirloom that once was
drug paraphernalia, but *is*

a silver spoon
nonetheless. We be the bougie,
uppity negroes.
We know what the old block is *saying*,

that we, the children of welfare and wreckage,
of sugar water and government cheese,
forgot where we came from.
That

"we don't know nobody no mo'."
That our houses and our attitudes are brand new.
We know that
these

new neighbors of ours,
with their gold gardens and teatimes,
ain't fond of us. But now we are
envied by our own *people*.

We thought making it out was everybody's dream.
Never cared to ask
about the nightmares
of those who *do*.

We know what our white neighbors call us
when they are alone.
It is the exact thing we tell our children
we will *not*

call ourselves.
We know when Black folks drive by, they are surprised
to see us—
the Black and fortunate. *Ultimately*

we do not fit in their imaginations—smiling, cleaning gutters,
and tending to lawns that are our own,
with children and wives as Black as we are.
We did not *cease*

our contact with all we used to know.
We attend the baby showers and the homegoings,
the cookouts, and coming-homes from prison.
Laverne still goes *to*

Englewood to get her perm.
Daddy refuses to leave
his barber shop over East.
Where else would he *be*?

It's the children we worry about.
Bullied for speaking proper English.
or knowing when to
use them or *they*.

Called Oreo
for coming from two-parent-homes
and knowing their daddies,
and having mothers who *make*

bagged lunches,
PTO meetings, and 85K a year.
Teased for bringing home report cards
doused in *Excellent*,

gold stars, and stickers.
For not knowing the latest fashion
and having more friends in college courses
than as *corpses*

We thought y'all would celebrate us for finding refuge.
An enclave of Black excellence,
a kind of suburbia *among*

other Black folks
who had the smarts to leave the hood
but not the heart to leave Chicago.
Besides, *the*

commute to work from Crete would be too long,
and traveling back and forth to take care
of Momma too
expensive.

We won't apologize
for doing alright for ourselves
for giving our children more.
In Beverly our children can grow like the *flowers.*

FEBRUARY AT A WHITE SCHOOL

No Black
    Panther cosplay.
No *Jeopardy*-styled trivia games
or *Who Am I*

No Tubman. No Baker.
        No Truth.

No special assembly
     where everyone gathers
to lift every voice and sing.

No Du Bois. No Hamer. No Hughes.
      Not even in the syllabus.

No mentions of the firsts
      (unless it's Washington)
Not even an Obama
joke these days.

No red, black, and green
    just white
       and a little pink
for Valentine's day.

Just a pesky WASP
     for a roommate
       with his nest of dirty laundry,
and fried chicken in the cafeteria on Wednesdays.

EBONICS 101

Now perhaps I should start this poem
by informing you that I am bilingual.
The Queen's English that I speak
so eloquently before you now
is not my first language.
My grandmother never used such diction
when she spoke me up
in the welfare line amongst the other dwellers,
or when she called down
to me from the project window for dinner.
We spoke a more Southern-fried English.

This rhetorical recipe has been in my family for generations.
Grandma says, Big Mama hid it under her tongue as she headed
for Northern cities during a great migration. Scholars call it
African American Vernacular English.

My guys call it Slang. The Man calls it Ebonics.
I call it America's creole, the last remaining squab
birthed from a European and African pidgin.
Turned into the dialect of the dough boys,
the bass that appears in a rapper's rhythmic rhetoric
spoken everywhere from the trap house
to the liquor store, from the HIV testing clinic to the bus
stop.

Ebonics is the official language to the undefined Black culture,
the native tongue to the underrepresented Black American,
and long before I received liberal arts degrees and stood
unimposing in academic settings I born on the South Side of
Chicago, and managed to garner enough street cred
from the school of hard knocks to qualify me to teach you a few
of my language's essentials
So, hipsters, I hope you got your notepads ready.

This is Ebonics 101.

Chapter 1
In any English word that holds an *i-n* combination, the *i*
becomes an *a*
Examples:
Billie Holiday couldn't just sing, that girl could *sang*
If Martin did all that *walkin'* I wonder if him feet *stank*
Traveled all them miles just to hear freedom *rang*
I wonder what he was *thankin'*

Chapter 2
In any English word ending in *-r* or *-re*, the *r* sound becomes silent.
Examples:
Emmett screaming *don't beat me no mo'*
Rodney screaming *don't beat me no mo'*
Trayvon asking *what is you following me fo'*

Lesson 3
In any English word that holds an *-er* combination, the
combination becomes an *-a*
like in the great quote from the linguistics scholar
Ms. Lauryn Hill:
And even after all my logic and my theory I add a "Motherfucka"
so you ignorant niggas hear me.

See there's culture in these words,
the bent back of my speech
comes from years of carrying the Black experience.
The verbal diaspora of Africa shapes my spine

we cross our T's like middle passages
dot our I's with strange fruit,
curve ours S's like mid-Atlantic routes.

You cannot expect us to be slaves to your phonetics forever.
And just like our history we defy the structure of your Jim Crow
grammar,
refuse to speak within the lines of your Mason-Dixon diction.
You can't correct this, context this,
connotate my accomplishments.

See, me, be, Black, male.
Use double negative to make positive.

I will write until the Black struggle no longer subsists
I will write until a clenched pen is synonymous with a clenched fist
I will write till Black Male is able to live, breathe, exist.

Class dismissed.

EXODUS 20:12 KJV

for G'G

after Patricia Smith

Sometimes it was tacked on the tail
   end of a reprimand
      a final exclamation point
   in case I was fixin' to talk back.

Most times it came sandwiched
between a late-night news headline of loss
then a tsk, a sigh, a shaking of the head,
and a reminder we are in the last days.

I heard it said to my younger cousin Mya
after she grew
fast. When paternal words felt more like suggestions
      than commandments set in stone.

When grandmothers grew slower
and their backhands less fierce.
When we could no longer be threatened into submission
or be stared into repentance. Their hope
was that as we feared them less, we would fear God more.

I heard it as
a plea
a last gasp
before a parent let go
and let God.

I heard it in the testimony of prodigal sons
   who returned home from prison
or smoke the clouds of back alleys.

I heard it from preachers kids who fell
   victim to the spirit of rebellion and disobedience.

I heard it out of the mouth of my G'G
in eulogy
the summers those late-night news headlines had names
of people we knew.
I heard it as a warning to those who were left
who too may not live long.

TEMPERATURE CHECK

Each October my grandmother calls
to tell me she ain't

cooking for Thanksgiving this year.
How work ain't goin' good, how she tired, and how money is tight

She is known for her empty

threats.

Her hands don't know how not to
rip and steam and cut and bake.

She just calls to hear me
groan, grovel, and beg.

To hear me say how much I love her

cooking.

How ain't no banana puddin' like her banana puddin'
and *remember the last time we let Phyllis make the mac and cheese?*

This is nothing more than a temperature check.
To make sure I ain't forgot her

hands, and what they can do and make

like stuffing from scratch,

like cornbread with no Jiffy

like a way out of no way.

SECTION 2:

BLACK AND BLUE(S)

THE GANGSTA'S GHAZAL

I would kill for my niggas
I would steal for my niggas

If Big Homie say to let you slide
then I would chill for my niggas

We don't love these women
It's just a thrill for my niggas

They killed Malik big brotha'
So I did a drill for my niggas

I'm not saying I want to die
just saying I will for my niggas

THE BABY MAMAS (A SCENE).

after Patricia Smith

Hello?
Hello?
Hey this Terri? Got a baby by Ken?
Yeah, who this?
Hey girl this Monica. I'm KJ momma. Ken older son.
Oh hey. Yeah, hold on *(beat)* OK hello?
You busy girl? I can call back?
Nah you cool.
Yeah well, *(beat)* **KJ having a birthday party next weekend
and I wanted to see if you and yo son wanted to come. It's
superhero themed. Avengers. We gone have a playhouse and
candy bags for the kids.**
Oh, that's nice. When is it?
Next Saturday.
Oh alright. I got to work.
That's OK. I can pick him up *(beat)* **or Ken can bring him. He
supposed to be comin' to hook up the music.**
OK yeah, we can do that.
Yeah I didn't know if Ken told you but I figured I'd call you.
(beat) **Yo baby is my baby's brother and I feel like they should
know each other.**
Yeah.
They don't got nothing to do with their parents' mess.
True.
**My momma can come get him before you go to work. You can
bring him with a bag. He can spend a night**
OK. Yeah.
How old your baby now?
Three.
**I got some old clothes of KJ's if you want 'em. I know Ken
probably doing the bare minimum.**
Girl I barely see his ass.

I know it. (*laughs*) **Well I'mma send you back with some stuff**
OK. (*beat*) Thank you girl.
No problem girl. I know how it is. You not alone. (*beat*) **OK I'll**
let you go. See you Saturday.
Yes. I'll see you Saturday.

A SCOLDING FOR THE BROTHER, DYLANN

from the children of Mother Emanuel

Nice try, Dylann, but we are still
going to church.

Still gonna claim this
white man's religion, once

used to enslave us. Still
gonna fill these white pews with

Black plight. Still gonna hallelujah,
still gonna be

a nigga,
still gonna come as we are

in our Sunday's best,
casket ready. We still

gonna lift our voices to sing.
Despite the threat

our eyes are closed
and our heads bowed at benediction.

This is how we Bible study,
we communion,

how we love on
our enemies,

how we make a neighbor
out of a wretch

like me. I know why you chose here,
Dylann.

Mother has always been
a womb

for revolution,
an embryo of resistance.

But did you forget, we are also gentle
children of the Father,

Dylann? We don't mind an unexpected
trip home.

COPAGANDA

According to the Oxford Research Encyclopedia,
more than 300 police dramas have aired on American television
since 1950. The boom coinciding directly with America's political
appetite for Law and Order and a media-glamorized War on Drugs.

Fact: In order for any Black male entertainer to unsuspiciously enter
the homes of White American audiences, he must first be willing
to play a cop on TV. Never mind how unlikely this is. For him to be
typecast as cop before convict. This is entertainment. Made
for TV, and you are no longer Black but Blue.

Before Bill Cosby became America's favorite TV dad, he was
Alexander Scott, partner to Robert Culp, secret agent, and the first
accepted Black face in the primetime white gaze. 3 Emmys later
he uses his *I Spy* money to purchase Spanish Fly on the wall
and becomes America's most famous peeping Uncle Tom.

A year after wearing a red jumpsuit on a DC stage, Eddie Murphy
was in Beverly Hills investigating the murder of a white man
that the Detroit PD wouldn't, and that's all it took. From SNL's
Stevie Wonder skit, to badge, baton, blockbuster, boom.

Gangster rapper Ice-T traded in his Adidas that squeak for a pair of
boots worth licking. America's first OG turned NYPD, now the
Lifetime true story on how the man who wrote *6 in the Mornin*
became 12.

30 years later Amerikkkas Most Wanted, Ice Cube, will bring Kevin
Hart for a ride along, and for a 90-minute runtime we will all forget
to sing *fuck the police*.

Martin Lawrence and Will Smith will save the city of Miami *thrice*
yet in the collective consciousness we will know *them* as Bad Boys.

Shawn and Marlon Wayans were cops and White Chicks
simultaneously. Yet remarkably Terry Crews is the only nigga
to get shot.

Denzel Washington got the highest honor from the academy
when he was willing to show Ethan Hawke American policing done
the right way.

Don't you get it? This is war by Copaganda.
Turn your favorite Black radicals into Officer Friendly.
Offer them a seat in middle-class America with a pension
the size of a buddy cop film budget. Whitewash them in blue blood.
Convince you Kamala Harris is Claire Huxtable.
Trade a dark-skinned Aunt Viv in for a white Virginia and see
Clarence Thomas was always the real Uncle Phil.

Now give abuelita 20 more seasons of *Law and Order*.
Replay the same scenes on the news.
Tell her Dick Wolf wrote it
and that these are all true stories.

IMAGINED ETYMOLOGY #1

felony ('fɛləni)

origin: us

sounds like an expensive brand
Fendi, Prada, Gucci, Felony
Something every nigga got
on his wish list

The shit sounds flashy
Like an e class or an expensive watch
Busted down
Jammed
packed with so many rocks
Who gives a fuck about the time.

It could be one of those ghetto names
something yo BM thought up
for the baby. An homage to her aunties
Felicia and Melody who took over
after her momma got strung out.

(Might call her fe fe or ne ne for short)
Or a flower,

Momma thought you too beautiful for roses
so we littered your casket with felonies
as they lowered you into the ground.

I saved a few of the felonies from the repast
and made all our niggas take one home with them.

JOHN HENRY OF RUSTBELT (A FOLKLORE)

John Henry sat on poppa's knee
Said "a steel driving man I'll be"
John grabbed his hammer
Bosses grabbed the steam
They shipped John's steel job overseas

THE FIRST TIME A MAN ATTEMPTS TO FIGHT HIS FATHER
(A FLASH FICTION)

The first time a man attempts to fight his father, he will be
on the bitter end of 17. The challenge is
an unanticipated reaction to his father's disrespect.

He will approach slowly,
adjust his shoulder in preparation for battle
chin firm and lifted
cause ain't no man ever tangoed looking at his feet.
He will look his mother's husband dead
in the face, suck his teeth, and flare his nostrils
as if to say

> ain't gone be no mo' getting switches,
> ain't gone be no mo' cause I said so,
> no mo' cracking jokes at the barbershop at my expense,
> no mo' playful shrugs to the head and gone boy.

> nah,
> this ain't spontaneous.
> nah this ain't impulse,
> and i ain't lost my damn mind.
> This is premeditated,
> a well-calculated ambush
> in the name of my manhood,
> and no offense pops
> I just figured
> if we ever gone see eye to eye again
> its gone be this way
> face to face
> square stances
> and clenched fist.

The first time a man attempts to fight his father he will be
scared out of his mind
but can neither surrender nor retreat
a cock strong
buck of a nigga
a Black knight tired of playing
pawn
the first shot
will feel like a shotgun blast
in the center of his abdomen
he will recollect himself
only to be met by a second blow.
Who knew
that the same hand
that rocked your cradle
could slap fire from your ass?
The first time
won't be the last time
won't be the only time
that a bedroom becomes a boxing ring
that an uppercut will be justified by a Bible verse
to *never spare a rod or spoil the child*
to *train him up the way he should go*
for he does not depart from it.

'Cause a boy his age needs discipline
'cause a boy with his skin needs discipline
rather daddy do it
than the streets do it
than the system do it
than a crooked cop do it.
Pray each time a father's hands
turn to pistol or revolver

>   *that my son learns to*
>   *put his hands up*
>   *don't resist authority*

don't demand your dignity
don't fight for your manhood
treat their presence the way they treat yours
like a bearing of arms
lower your gaze if you got to
be a good boy
for however long you are in police custody
you are fighting a losing battle
in a stand your ground state
in a court of public opinion
you will go on trial for your own murder

the first time a man attempts to fight his father
is when you know he is
Man
is when you know he inherited his momma's no-bullshit policy
is when you know he got a little revolutionary in him
got that from his daddy side
is when you know he is feared
is when you know that plus his Black is the sum of their demonic
is when you know he's obituary ready
is when you know he protest worthy
is when you know he's target.

The first time.

COMRADE BROTHER HAMPTON ADDRESSES THE PEOPLE

Now, Somewhere a Black Capitalist lies
To himself. Says he is his ancestors'
Wildest dreams cause he got a four-wheel drive
And a house as big as the oppressor.
These folks think we died on the plantation
Wishing for our own field of niggas. To hold
Bags of cotton ain't emancipation.
What profits a slave with Carolina Gold?
We dreamed of no whips, no work, no white men
No U.S.A. & death as life redeemed.
We ain't dream of havin' Black masters when
Our bodies collapsed at night. We ain't dream
Of stocks or corporations with our names
But of freedom, and the Big House in flames.

ODE TO THE BOYS WHO DIE TO MAKE HIP HOP HAPPEN

Before this poem's end
this wound will drain and expand
and my cease heartbeat
will bleed into instrumental

Shame I had to die
just to get my life on track/
I was dippin caught/slippin
now my lifes on wax.
But don't feel sorry for me
the opps caught me hangin
off the 9 when
Click click bang bang
I was chief keefed
adlibbed into the afterlife/ but ain't that your favorite part
of the song when Bobby catches the body
if you listen closely
you can hear my body drop
before the beat does/

and no we never intended to be
the muses to the worlds'
most popular music
just got a feel for that shit/
us baby face savages that were already born **the notorious**
and ready to die/ &
cute enough for album covers
the stroke brings us wrapped
in rags and parental advisory stickers/so here I am God
a sacrifice for the culture
ready my soul's release date
to be placed on an eternal stream/forever laid to rest in a casket
colored cassette/I can hear it now

my demise gonna be the most requested at all the parties
tell Big Mama her baby boy got his own hymn now

Mama freed the base now I'm the boom
Daddy sipped the liquor now I'm a bar
that's not no record scratch that's just me trying to crawl up out this
casket, trying to unzip this body bags, so I can join Nipsey I can hear
them now 'cause I can hear them scream

imma hit imma hit imma hit imma imma hit imma hit imma
hit imma hit imma hit imma hit im hit hit im hit im hit im hit
im hit im hit im

THE LEGITIMATES' VILLANELLE

We don't judge him for what he did
We just hate the way that we found out
That Daddy had other kids

Who knows what else he hid
Stepping out on Momma roaming about
We don't judge him for what he did

My brother couldn't believe it, he blew his lid
But Uncle Roy said he could vouch
That Daddy had other kids

He was always on the run and off the grid
And him and the girl favor, ain't no doubt
We don't judge him for what he did

I wonder if Momma hated Daddy just a tid-
bit. I've never seen her whine nor pout
That Daddy had other kids

But to get a cut of the money, that I forbid
This Illegitimate with her hand out
We don't judge him for what he did
That Daddy had other kids

MOMMA SAYS, "GO WHEREVER YOU WANT FOR COLLEGE, JUST STAY OUT OF THE SOUTH"

I don't know how to tell
Momma
the South is everywhere.

The South is rural
towns
and urban cities.

The South is below
the Mason-Dixon line
and above it.

The South is over East
the Midwest
and the West coast.

The South is coal mines and cotton fields
or wherever there are red-
wood forests or spacious skies.

The South is Paris,
London, Dublin, and Madrid.

The South is right here
in your living room,
in your kitchen,
even in your embrace,

Momma,
the South is anywhere
and everywhere
the **slave** is standing.

IMAGINED ETYMOLOGY #9

23 and 1 ('twɛnti θri ænd wʌn)

origin: hell

Makes me think of gambling
a brand of slot machine

Big Mama's favorite thing to play when she go to "The Boat"

Fuck craps, fuck Blackjack. Fuck Texas
Hold em. I'm at 23 and 1

Betting BIG

On the block we only let the real niggas play
23 and 1. It's a man's game

HOW THE HOOD LOVES YOU BACK

I watched a group of men pour malt liquor in the cracked throat
of pavement in the name of eulogy,
then pack the back of a stolen jalopy strapped
with black market arsenal and intoxicated vengeance.
I scanned the nightly news in anticipation of hearing gunshots
protrude the silence of a Chicago summer night.

They did,
and I left the porch light on for 'em.
Now, I'm not saying I agree with what they did.
I'm just saying I've learned not to judge a people
for how they grieve,
learned not to judge the Hood
for how it loves you back.

Love from the Hood,
an honor only bestowed on those who showed the Hood
the most unwavering loyalty. I'm talking street niggas.
Most literally, from cradle to grave.
Most literally, from corner to coroner.
Most literally, niggas who hugged the block
in their last moments, gasping for air
right before yellow tape made a spectacle of their body
sprawled on cement.

If the Hood loves you
she'll make a monument of this site.
She will bring teddy bears, well wishes, and heavy hearts.
This is now sacred ground
to be renamed as memorial and landmark.
This is no longer Jefferson Avenue
but where Twig got shot.

For the next six nights you see the candles light this space holy
until the wind blows it silent,
until its ember blows in the direction of the summer's next casualty.

If the Hood loves you, she'll write it in tombstone text,
a boy's face and childhood nickname will be written in script
across a XXL white tee.

Ain't it funny, how quickly death becomes fashionable,
a testament to how tragic memories don't fade
even in the washing machine.

You can expect your closest of kin to tattoo your name
in the most visible of places.
Your birthdate in Roman numerals
will kiss the left side of your little sister's collarbone
long before a boy ever does.

In grief we graffiti murals;
that's how Biggie and Pac got faces in places
they never called home.

I know boys who've borne the weight of pallbearer
long before the rigors of college.
But the most famous of us will have streets
named in our honor.

Martin Luther King Drive and Malcolm X Boulevard
both debunk the myth of respectability
and prove that, no matter the politics,
all Black boys are doomed to die
from bullets.
But how can you complain?
When the Hood loves you.

And we gone keep loving you,
long after the gravel has swallowed your portion of the 40,

long after they packed that car with vengeance,
long after another boy's life is taken in retaliation of yours
continuing the cycle of trauma and street violence.

Yes y'all, the Hood will love you enough to murder for you
but never enough to snitch.
Yes y'all, I know who did it, I was there
when they bought the four 5th
Yes y'all, I watched the news;
I listened as they emptied the clip.
Yes y'all, I'll do it again.
Yes y'all, I'll do it again.
Damn mother fucking right I'll do it again,
because I miss my brother so much.
But that don't mean that I agreed with what they did,
just means I've learned not to judge a people for how they grieve.
Learned not to judge the Hood for how it loves you back.

IMAGINED ETYMOLOGY #12

sentence (ˈsɛntəns)

origin: the ocean

something constantly moving
not to be stopped or controlled

I can hear my niggas saying they hate sentencing

they say *that's some white people shit*,
like water rafting or snowboarding

sounds like another way to die

and niggas already got enough ways to die

to now just go

and add sentencing to it.

For those who do go they always return
with grand stories of the sentence

O' how vast it is,

O' how consuming

O' how it changes you.

WALLACE ASKS WHY WE CALL IT "THE PIT" (A MONOLOGUE)

D'Angelo Barksdale:

ever seen a fiend after he spark?

all mouth
eyes flickering
the body sways & waves

like fire

the fiend is a flame
and this is where we control the fire
where we feed the flame.

but make sure
you watch 'em.
get too close
and they'll come up running
with a hand full of coffee-
stained monopoly money
looking to burn you.

that's why you carry heat
you got to
let him know
you not scared
to catch a 1st, 2nd, or 3rd
    degree

charge off this shit.
got to fight fire with fire.

us D boys
we like the first
cavemen really
for how we discovered fire.

folks like to say we made
this shit
but nah
we just uncovered
what was already there.

a bunch of niggas in the dark
looking for a light.

we just serve
the light.

shit
the fiends get the better
bargain if you ask me.

they can just quit
leave the pit.
only way out for us

is to get smoked.

AN HONEST QUESTION

How many 3/5s
Of a Human Does it Take
To start a Riot

DOGGONE

They say a Pitbull ain't nothing but
the Black man of the canine kingdom

and Poodles clutch their leash
when they pass him on the street

Golden retrievers growl
their microaggressions on the job

when out for a walk German Shepherds
stop sniff and frisk him

Forever stuck to face the stereotypes
of his breed

Does he belong to drug dealers?
                                        Does he participate in dogfights?
Is he angry
                        is his vicious tendency innate
or a product of his environment?

I swear they liked us better
when we were The Man's best friend

when we were being bred
for our ability and our strength

and they wonder why we riot
they wonder why we
                knock over the bowl
                        and bite the hand that fed us
scraps

you made us this way
and now you kitty cat scared?

Funny how bullets stray like dogs
whenever I disobey
a cop's command

and now Fox News asks my momma all the doggone questions like

Why didn't he sit?   *Why didn't he stay?*

Why wasn't he a good boy?

POLICE AS PANTOUMS #1 (INTERROGATION)

For the Central Park 5

Officer 1

What do you know about the rape
The sooner you tell us what you know the sooner you can go home
This isn't a game
We need some answers

Officer 2

The sooner you tell us what you know the sooner you can go home
They say you did it
We need some answers
Who were you with?

Officer 1

They say you did it
You telling us you did nothing
Who were you with
Where did you see the lady

Officer 2

You telling me you did nothing
What do you know about the rape
Where did you see the lady
This isn't a game.

POLICE AS PANTOUMS #27 (TRAFFIC STOP)

(*Places hand on gun*)
Gonna ask you to keep your hands on the steering wheel for me.
                                        Where you headed?
Is this your vehicle?

Gonna ask you to keep your hands on the steering wheel for me.
                        Anything in the car I should know about?
                                        Is this your vehicle?
                Relax, guy, you are making me nervous.

                        Anything in the car I should know about?
                        Any weapons on ya?
        Relax, guy, you are making me nervous.
                        (*into radio*) 11-96 on Crenshaw and Melrose.

Any weapons on ya?
                        (*Officer unholsters gun*)
(*into radio*) 11-96 Crenshaw and Melrose.
                        Move again. I dare you.

IMAGINED ETYMOLOGY #29

mass incarceration (mæs ɪnˌkɑrsəˈreɪʃən)

origin: USA

Makes me think of the babies,
this for them. They get it young.

Pacifiers, Pampers and Incarcerations.

Uncle Sam brought some to the baby shower as a gift.

My momma kept mine in good shape
so she could pass my incarceration down to my brother.

You know incarcerations are expensive.
If you treat em right they can last

years.

maybe it's something to keep
folks in America safe.

as in: *My guns and my incarcerations will protect me*

Little kid ask *how many incarcerations you got*

I say, not enough,
cause you can never have too many
and they're my God
given constitutional right

THE DEAD UNARMED BLACK MAN THE POLICE SHOT
LAST WEEK HAD A FUNERAL TODAY

and everybody showed up except me.
You remember me right?
I'm the dead unarmed Black man.

Guess everybody got so caught up in their own passions
they ain't notice
I never arrived.

Oh no, don't be alarmed,
there's a body in that casket,
it's just not mine.
It's whatever the media made of me
after you noosed me
in narratives: *good kid/mad city.*
Whichever sells your newspapers faster.

You know I never even made it to the afterlife.
Just stuck in this political purgatory
where they swap out hashtags for halos
and give picket signs for tombstones
Now people speak of me like I never was flesh
Just myth, a legend, a folklore, just a cautionary tale
Black parents tell their Black sons
of what happens when you aren't careful
around police.

I guess I should thank y'all though, right?
'Cause of you I'll never die.
Why rest in peace when you can rest in thinkpieces?
Have your name spoken in italics by all the slam poets.
The mayor will use my story as anecdote in her call for gun reform.

Fuck this fake ass funeral!

Got the so-called political dignitaries in the front
and my niggas in the back
a pulpit full of self-proclaimed revolutionaries
confusing my casket for a soapbox
for them to stand on.
I mean, fuck, did you ask my Mama
if she wanted any of this?
No. You just shoved a microphone in her face
and told her tell story
told her to use platform.
And what's her platform?

me?
my body?
her grief?

Y'all wanna do something for me?
Just let my homies know
I ain't go out like no punk iight.
That I ain't just let no pig cap me.
That I went down swinging.
That he only grabbed the heat
'cause I was getting the best of him.
He wasn't used to a nigga like me
so he had to grab the gun
cause he couldn't take these hands,
and my OG always told me watch a nigga hands
when you scrap and I didn't,
and that's my fault but stop with all that political bullshit.
My death was neither justified nor genocide
I am not the right's monster
or the left's martyr.
I was no good kid
or no lost cause.
I'm just dead.
I'm gone,
'cause some cop couldn't handle the smoke.

MOMMA SAYS WE SHOULD PRAY BEFORE WE LEAVE FOR THE PROTEST

You have left us in the hands of these devils.
So we have replaced you with more avenging gods.
Horus. Isis. Oshun. The Gun.

I do not doubt we were made in your image.
They too have made ritual of feasting on our bodies.
We too have been the Eucharist for white masses.

Without your heaven as a consolation,
what reason do I have in waiting?

There is no reason for us to fear
hell. We are already a city engulfed in flames.

NO BLACK BOYS DIE ON MOTHER'S DAY

And there the Church Mothers go again,
herding their grandbabies into church pews
like a shepherd preparing for a storm.
The oldest is bribed by the promise of dinner,
its greens and its pot liquor.
The youngest, a purse's bottomless pit
of peppermint candies.
But hey, we all *here*.
Now, I don't know what the CME
in Bethel Temple CME church stands for,
but I imagine it stands for Christmas, Mother's Day, and Easter:
the Holy Trinity of Black religious celebration.
The only days that we, the biological descendants
of this church's mothers,
are forced to be here.

And today is Mother's Day,
the most sacred of the three.
The only day that the Black matriarch
can get even her grown son to flaunt
hot pink and a blazer.
Loafers and slacks are a tall order, she knows,
so she'll settle for him in white sneakers and jeans.
If he won't wear a belt,
hopefully he can hold his pants up long enough
that they don't fall during the altar call.
It doesn't matter what you wear, she says,
come as you are. All that matters is that you are here

And we are all here,
under the watchful eye of the lord
and a grandmother in the choir stand.

We
the proof of our grandmother's blessing.

                    We
the evidence that the prayers of the righteous availeth much

We
the barrage of belligerent Black boys

who stand on your street corners
and tote vendettas and berettas
on May's second Saturday

only to tote Bibles and bowties
on May's second Sundays.

On Mother's Day,
we will come as we are

with no street cred
but that of our grandmother's last tithe.

We will come as we are

with no reputation
but that of our grandmother's last testimony.

And our grandmothers will pack the congregation with us

as if to say:
look what the Lord has done

how he's been faithful

how he's kept them
                                                    alive.
And ain't it just like a Black woman
to have a day dedicated to her
but spend it praying for somebody else.

And today nobody gets jammed up out West
no turf wars happen over East
no police go acquitted up North.

Today the block is quiet.
Today the morgue is empty.
Today the jailhouse chatter has fallen
to a sweet mutter of *Mama*

'cause the truth is no Black boys die
on Mother's Day.

We all here
among our grandmothers'
hymns hats and hallelujahs,
our blunt-blistered lips
touch cheek to make kiss
before our heads bow to pray.

And I know, Mama.

I know with all that's going on in this world
it gets harder to get us all together like this.
But you managed it this year,
and we all here.

We
are all here

IMAGINED ETYMOLOGY #18

innocence ('ɪnəsəns)

origin: god

makes me think of birds.
something regal, strong, or fierce

something you'd see as a sports team logo
or
on a country's money
or
a statue outside of an important building

a creature fitted for a poet's best metaphor

a Greek god
a sun of Zeus

a protagonist of its own

Myth.

ABOUT THE AUTHOR

Performance Poet and playwright Steven Antoine Willis mixes elements of hip hop poetics and theatrical performance with formal teachings of anthropology and political theory to help express his eclectic personal narrative. Willis is a contributing writer to *The BreakBeat Poets: New American Poetry in the Age of Hip-Hop* Anthology, National Council for Teachers of English Journal, is a 3-time Individual World Poetry Slam finalist and former multi-time slam team member of the Nuyorican Poets Café. Willis received his MFA in Acting from the University of Iowa in 2021. He currently attends Iowa Writers Workshop for poetry.

OTHER BOOKS BY BUTTON POETRY

If you enjoyed this book, please consider checking out some of our others, below. Readers like you allow us to keep broadcasting and publishing. Thank you!

Neil Hilborn, *Our Numbered Days*
Hanif Abdurraqib, *The Crown Ain't Worth Much*
Sabrina Benaim, *Depression & Other Magic Tricks*
Rudy Francisco, *Helium*
Rachel Wiley, *Nothing Is Okay*
Neil Hilborn, *The Future*
Phil Kaye, *Date & Time*
Andrea Gibson, *Lord of the Butterflies*
Blythe Baird, *If My Body Could Speak*
Desireé Dallagiacomo, *SINK*
Dave Harris, *Patricide*
Michael Lee, *The Only Worlds We Know*
Raych Jackson, *Even the Saints Audition*
Brenna Twohy, *Swallowtail*
Porsha Olayiwola, *i shimmer sometimes, too*
Jared Singer, *Forgive Yourself These Tiny Acts of Self-Destruction*
Adam Falkner, *The Willies*
George Abraham, *Birthright*
Omar Holmon, *We Were All Someone Else Yesterday*
Rachel Wiley, *Fat Girl Finishing School*
Bianca Phipps, *crown noble*
Rudy Francisco, *I'll Fly Away*
Natasha T. Miller, *Butcher*
Kevin Kantor, *Please Come Off-Book*
Ollie Schminkey, *Dead Dad Jokes*
Reagan Myers, *Afterwards*
L.E. Bowman, *What I Learned From the Trees*
Patrick Roche, *A Socially Acceptable Breakdown*
Andrea Gibson, *You Better Be Lightning*
Rachel Wiley, *Revenge Body*
Ebony Stewart, *BloodFresh*
Ebony Stewart, *Home.Girl.Hood.*
Kyle Tran Mhyre, *Not A Lot of Reasons to Sing, but Enough*

Available at buttonpoetry.com/shop and more!

FORTHCOMING BOOKS BY BUTTON POETRY

Topaz Winters, *So, Stranger*
Siaara Freeman, *Urbanshee*
Junious 'Jay' Ward, *Composition*
Darius Simpson, *Never Catch Me*
Robert Lynn, *How to Maintain Eye Contact*